FIRST FIELD GUIDE TO
SKYWATCHING
IN SOUTHERN AFRICA

GW00402013

NASA

*Venus, the evening
star (page 31)*

The magnificent Orion Nebula (page 23)

CLIFF TURK

Contents

Published by Struik Nature (an imprint of Penguin Random House (Pty) Ltd)
Reg. No. 1953/00041/07
The Estuaries No 4, Oxbow Crescent, Century Avenue, Century City, 7441
PO Box 1144, Cape Town, 8000
South Africa

Visit www.randomstruik.co.za and join the Struik Nature Club for updates, news, events, and special offers.

First edition published in 2001
Second edition 2015
3 5 7 9 10 8 6 4 2

Publishing manager: Pippa Parker
Editor: Helen de Villiers
Designers: Janice Evans, Neil Bester
Illustrations: Steven Felmore, Dominic Robson

Reproduction by
Hirt & Carter Cape (Pty) Ltd
Printed and bound by
Times Offset (M) Sdn Bhd

ISBN 978 1 77584 389 4
ePub: 978 1 77584 390 0
ePDF: 978 1 77584 391 7

Introduction

The night skies of the southern hemisphere are by far the most interesting for astro-nomers, amateur and professional alike. From the southern hemisphere we can see many features that are too far south to be seen by northern hemisphere stargazers: the brightest parts of the Milky Way, the brightest stars, the brightest and biggest globular clusters[G] are all in the southern hemisphere. The south also has the two Magellanic Clouds, which are the most easily observable of the external galaxies; the nearer ones are obscured behind parts of the Milky Way.

The southern skies are less observed than those of the northern hemisphere. This is partly because there is less land and much more sea in the south, so it is physically impossible to have as many astronomers. As a result there is a greater chance of a southern astronomer making a discovery without being beaten to it by someone else. There are simply not enough professionals to cover everything; so keen amateurs have prospects of an exceptionally rewarding hobby.

This book is intended to provide enough knowledge to

The centre of the Milky Way, or galactic centre, is in the southern sky.

give confidence to those who start off feeling a little lost. It cannot be comprehensive, but covers a wide range of basics on which amateurs can build. Hopefully it will also provide a quick reference source for those more established.

There are many astronomical societies and interest groups – see 'Clubs and observatories' on page 54. Books are available that explain general principles applicable to both hemispheres, as well as those that apply just to our southern hemisphere – for more information see 'Further reading' on page 55.

Practical stargazing

The best way to familiarise yourself with the night sky is to step outside and look above you – on a regular basis. You will see many objects, some twinkling, some apparently static; occasionally there is something moving steadily across the sky and sometimes things even appear as whizzing and fading streaks of light. And of course there is the Moon.

By far the most numerous of all the objects are stars, and it may at first seem a daunting task to begin to identify and recognise specific stars and constellations[G]. The secret is to start slowly, with the aim of learning to recognise no more than two or three objects in the sky each night.

To start with, it is best to use just the naked eye, as optical aids increase the number of stars and other objects so dramatically that it is easy to get lost. You will eventually want to see some of the objects beyond the ability of the naked eye, and then the best option is binoculars (see page 9).

Star charts
Star charts or maps are essential aids to finding and identifying stars. These charts plot the stars and constellations[G] against a contrasting background, and show the night skies at a given time of the year. A set of star charts, one for each month of the year, appears on pp. 42–53. Before using the charts outside, spend some time indoors studying them. Use a soft pencil to identify shapes to look for when outside. A 2B pencil, used lightly, can be erased easily, leaving the charts still usable.

To use a star chart, it is necessary to orientate yourself with the main compass points. This is best achieved with a simple compass, remembering that it will point to magnetic north (or south), which are about 20° to 25° to the left

---

DARK ADAPTING

Your eyes take some 20 minutes or longer to become fully accustomed to the dark. Torch light (needed to read the charts) can hinder this process and it is better to use a red-light torch, which will not interfere with dark adaptation. Red cellophane or a piece of red plastic, cut to size and fitted in place of the torch's clear glass disk, works well.

of the true directions. This magnetic variation changes with your location and from year to year.

The moving sky

The relative positions of the stars are for all practical purposes fixed at a given time, and if an astronomer from 2,000 years ago were to see the sky tonight, he would recognise all his favourite constellations[G]. Individual movement of the stars is negligible, but the movement of the whole night sky further to the west from one night to the next is due to the Earth's orbit around the Sun.

The planets (see page 29), however, do move against the starry background, all at different speeds. The Moon also moves independently of the background. For this reason, the Moon and planets are not plotted in star atlases. If you want to locate the planets it is worthwhile getting an annual handbook (see 'Further reading', page 55), which contains a diary of events showing when the Moon is north or south of the brighter stars and planets, as it moves across the sky.

At night, the Moon and stars appear to be crossing the sky from east to west because of the Earth's rotation on its axis, but the Moon moves more slowly than the stars, so from our perspective the stars overtake it.

Close conjunctions[G] of solar system objects often make interesting photographs. This one shows the Moon with planets Venus (top left) and Jupiter.

As the sky moves a little further to the west each night, it is best to start learning to identify stars, clusters, constellations[G] and nebulae[G] from the eastern part of the sky. These objects will then remain in the sky for some months, allowing you to become really familiar with them. Meanwhile, new objects will continue to appear and climb upwards from the eastern horizon. Don't make the mistake of trying to observe too low down towards the horizon as the atmosphere there is thicker and will obscure many objects; in addition, city lights may reduce visibility. It is wise to start looking 30° or more above the horizon.

Glare from Cape Town's lights (seen from 200km away) obscures many stars in the sky.

STARS OR PLANETS?

It is not always obvious which bodies are planets and which are stars, but certain indicators can help us to distinguish one from the other.

- Planets move relative to the fixed background of stars – usually much faster than the stars.
- Planets, being vastly closer to Earth than any stars (with the exception of our Sun), appear to be fractionally larger than the stars, which look to us like very tiny point lights. Seen through Earth's atmosphere, starlight can appear to come and go, or to twinkle, whereas that of planets generally seems to be a more steady glow. To be sure, it is best to familiarise yourself with the night skies throughout the year and to learn the relative positions of different constellations[G] and the planets in our solar system.

Starhopping

Betelgeuse

Bellatrix

Orion's belt

Rigel

From the north, Orion appears upright, but we see it upside down.

Using one known part of the sky to help point you to another part is known as starhopping and it is probably the most useful skill you can acquire.

Orion and the Southern Cross are probably the two best-known constellations[G], and by far the easiest to locate in the southern skies, so it is a good idea to start with them. Orion is best located in summer, and the Southern Cross in winter.

Navigating the skies

Orion is high in the sky during the southern hemisphere summer when the Southern Cross is low on the southern horizon. Use the sky charts on pages 42 to 53 to locate either of these two constellations[G] and then watch their movements in the upcoming months.

Orion moves a little further towards the west each night; the belt always rises due east and sets due west. By about May it will start to disappear from the night sky, to reappear in about October.

ARTIFICIAL SATELLITES

Artificial satellites litter our skies and are often seen during an observing session. Because satellites must be illuminated by sunlight to be visible, they are most often seen in the western sky in the evening, and in the east in the early morning. Most travel from west to east, as the earth's rotation is used to help their launch velocity, but some can be seen in a polar orbit (moving north or south). Satellites are trapped in orbit, and appear as slow-moving 'stars' in the sky; they are not seen as rapid streaks of light and so shouldn't be confused with meteors[G].

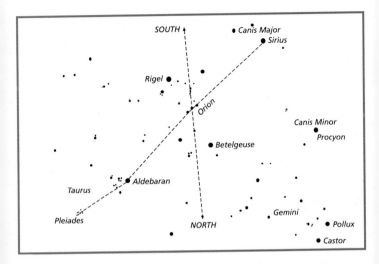

The Southern Cross, followed by its 'pointers', moves clockwise around a circle on the southern horizon and rises to some 60 degrees[G] above it.

Once you know where to find Orion straddling the equator in summer, you can follow the line of his belt northwestwards (down to the left) to a bright red star called Aldebaran – and you have found the eye of Taurus, the Bull! At that point you will also see the V-shape of the Bull's face with Aldebaran at one end of the V. Move your eyes the same distance again in the same direction and

you will find the open cluster[G] Pleiades (or Seven Sisters) located at the back of the Bull's neck.

Return to Orion, and move the other way along the belt, up to the right, towards the southeast, and you cannot miss Sirius, the brightest star in the sky – and the eye of Canis Major, the Great Dog. From there, move straight down to the north (parallel with Orion) and you have found Procyon, the Little Dog Star.

In acquiring this technique, you will gradually learn to navigate the night sky – perhaps to spot a newly discovered comet.

Viewing equipment

Binoculars

There are several advantages in using binoculars rather than a telescope when you start observing the night skies, not least of which is being able to use both eyes instead of only one. Binoculars are easier to handle and are also useful for a range of other activities, whereas an astronomical telescope – which inverts its image – is of little use for any other activity.

centre focusing   eyepiece focusing

object lens

Binoculars are essential for stargazing.

Binoculars are specified by a pair of numbers, such as 7 x 50, which indicates that they magnify seven times, and that the object lenses are 50mm in diameter. Other sizes may be 8 x 30 or 10 x 40, and so on. For astronomy you need the biggest object lenses possible in order to gather the greatest amount of light from faint objects. Magnification[G] is much less important. If you magnify too much, it becomes difficult to hold the binoculars steady. Some consider 10 x 50 to be the ideal choice, but many astronomers prefer the lower magnification[G] power of 7 x 50.

Focusing correctly

First cover the right object lens and focus for the left eye, using only the centre focusing wheel. Next cover the left side and do *not* touch the centre focusing wheel, but focus for the right eye, using only the separate adjuster on that eyepiece. Now the two halves of the binoculars are preset for any difference between the user's eyes. Adjust the width between the two barrels of the binoculars to suit the distance between your eyes.

The right eyepiece adjuster and the centre hinge are usually provided with scales and it is a good idea to note where you have them so that you can reset quickly for your own eyes if someone else has been using your binoculars. You should see a single, circular field of view.

Telescopes

The two basic types of telescope are refractors and reflectors. Refractors use lenses, whereas reflectors use mirrors for their main light-collecting surfaces. Refractors collect light on a lens specially designed from two pieces of glass, to make light of all wavelengths focus at the same point. A second lens (eyepiece) is then used to magnify the image formed at that point.

Reflectors use a concave mirror instead of a lens to make the rays of parallel light converge to a point. A second mirror is then used to divert the focus away from the incoming light path so that use of the eyepiece does not block the light. There are several types of reflectors and various mountings for them, but two basic types are the Newtonian and the Cassegrain. Each type has advantages. It is strongly advised that you try out other people's telescopes to check suitability before deciding which type to buy.

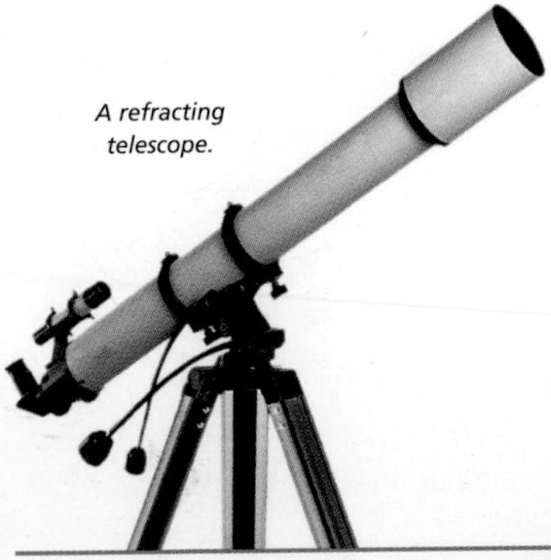

The refractor

eyepiece

white light

object lens

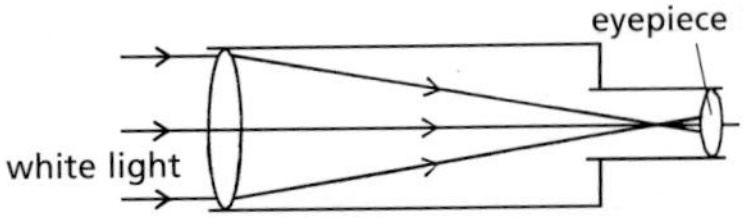

The Newtonian reflector

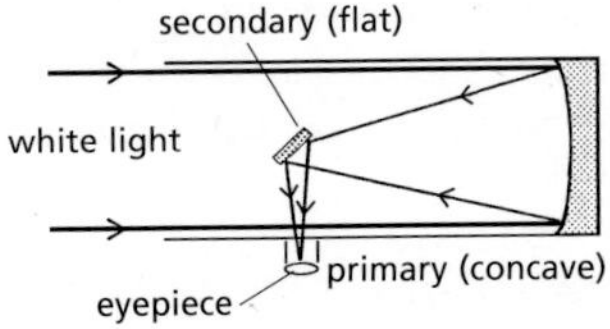

secondary (flat)

white light

primary (concave)

eyepiece

A refracting telescope.

The Cassegrain reflector

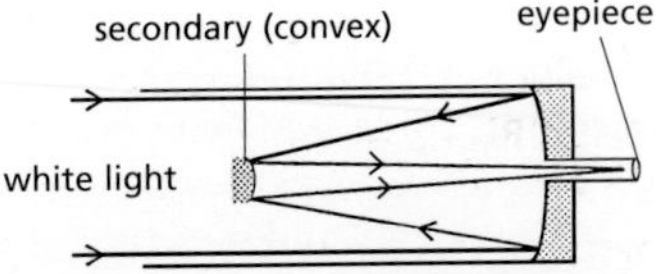

secondary (convex)

eyepiece

white light

primary (concave)

The celestial sphere

To identify the positions of particular stars, astronomers use a grid system just like that of longitude and latitude on Earth. Imagine the sky as a sphere surrounding the Earth, with all the stars 'stuck' on to it. The imaginary North and South poles are immediately above the Earth's poles. Similarly, directly above the Earth's equator is the celestial equator. The angular distance of a star from the celestial equator is measured in degreesG of arc (equivalent to latitude on the Earth's surface) and is called its Declination (Dec). A star at -34° Dec (minus because it is south of the equator) will pass directly over Cape Town, whose latitude is 34° south.

The celestial equivalent of longitude is called Right Ascension (RA). Every celestial object can be located by its values of RA and Dec.

A 20-minute photographic exposure shows the stars rotating around a central point. At the centre is the South Celestial Pole, which is directly above the Earth's South Pole.

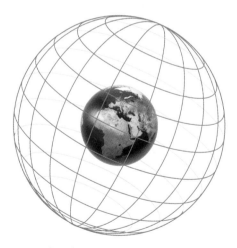

Lines of Right Ascension and Declination on the celestial sphere are the equivalent of longitude and latitude on Earth.

Right Ascension is more complicated than longitude on Earth, however, because the rotation of the Earth on its own axis and its simultaneous orbit around the Sun causes these imaginary lines to 'move' along with the stars from east to west (at a rate of about 15° per hour).

The apparent motion of the stars is in effect like a giant clock, and RA is measured eastwards – not in degrees[G], minutes[G] and seconds[G] like Declination, but in hours, minutes[G] and seconds[G] of time (24 hours corresponds to a full Earth rotation of 360° and 1° of RA = 4 minutes[G] of time).

The celestial sphere

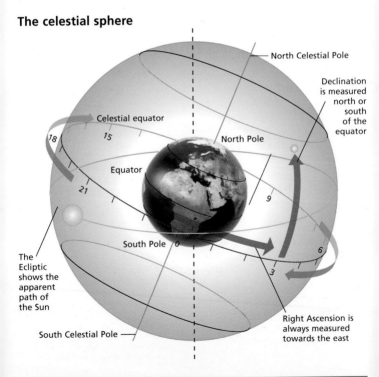

North Celestial Pole

Declination is measured north or south of the equator

Celestial equator

North Pole

Equator

South Pole

The Ecliptic shows the apparent path of the Sun

Right Ascension is always measured towards the east

South Celestial Pole

Measuring the sky

As all the objects in the sky look as if they are stuck to a giant dome above us, the easiest way to describe their relative positions is to use the angles between them. We can use angles to specify separations in any direction – not just along the lines of Right Ascension and Declination.

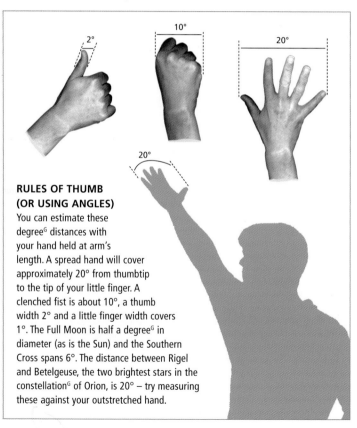

RULES OF THUMB (OR USING ANGLES)
You can estimate these degree^G distances with your hand held at arm's length. A spread hand will cover approximately 20° from thumbtip to the tip of your little finger. A clenched fist is about 10°, a thumb width 2° and a little finger width covers 1°. The Full Moon is half a degree^G in diameter (as is the Sun) and the Southern Cross spans 6°. The distance between Rigel and Betelgeuse, the two brightest stars in the constellation^G of Orion, is 20° – try measuring these against your outstretched hand.

Distances in space

Light years[G] and parsecs[G]

The enormous distances in astronomy make it impractical to talk about distances in kilometres. Much larger units are needed, and the best-known one is the light year[G] (ly). This is defined as the distance that light will travel (at approximately 300,000km per second) in one earth year. That is: 300,000 x 60 x 60 x 24 x 365, or about 9.5 million million kilometres.

An even larger unit is the parsec[G] (pc), which is equal to 3.26 light years[G], or the kiloparsec (kpc), which is one thousand parsecs[G].

Our Milky Way galaxy[G] is 100,000 light years[G] from edge to edge, and 5,000 light years[G] thick.

The pointers to the Southern Cross (above, to the left of the picture) appear close together – but one is actually 100 times further away than the other.

Star proximity

Two stars that appear close together in the night sky (for instance in the same constellation[G]) may be a vast distance apart in reality – they simply fall within the same line of sight when seen from the Earth. An example being the two stars Alpha and Beta Centauri, the pointers to the Southern Cross. Alpha Centauri is only 4.2 light years[G] distant and is the nearest star to the Sun, but Beta Centauri is about 100 times further away.

Finding south by the stars

Once you have a basic familiarity with the stars, you can use them to find your bearings without a compass, even in unfamiliar terrain. To find south very roughly, remember that the Sun rises in the east and sets in the west. When you have located the Southern Cross in the southern skies, there are three easy methods to help you find due south:

① Find the long axis of the Cross and extend it by four-and-a-half times its length in the direction of its longest point. This brings you to within about 3° of the South Celestial Pole. South is directly below this on the horizon.

② Draw an imaginary line from the long axis of the Cross directly across the sky to Achernar (the only bright star in the vicinity). Midway along this imaginary line is the South Celestial Pole.

③ A line drawn midway (and at right angles) between the Pointers to the Southern Cross intersects with the line from the long axis of the Cross at the South Celestial Pole.

Using any of these methods, you can locate the Pole – unless the Southern Cross is too low on the horizon or even out of sight in summer.

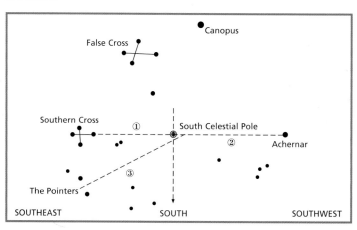

The brightness of the stars

The actual brightness of an object in the sky cannot be directly observed. What we see is called the apparent brightness or magnitude, which is determined both by the object's true brightness and by its distance from us. An inverse square law applies – any given star, if it were twice as far away, would appear one quarter as bright.

Early astronomers used a scale ranging from magnitude 1, for the brightest stars, to magnitude 6, for the faintest ones that could be seen with the naked eye. The brightest objects thus had the lowest magnitude numbers, and those that were dimmer had higher values. Measurements with an accuracy of thousandths of a magnitude have now replaced these visual estimates, and the scale has been defined so that magnitude 1 is 100 times as bright as magnitude 6. The difference in brightness between any two adjacent magnitudes is a factor of 2.5.

With the help of a good star atlas, a couple of hours under a really dark sky (with no Moon and away from artificial light) will give anyone a good grasp of stellar magnitudes.

The ten brightest stars

	Star	Constellation	Apparent mag.	Distance
1	Sun		-26.72	8.3 min
2	Sirius	Canis Major	-1.44	8.6 ly
3	Canopus	Carina	-0.72	312 ly
4	Rigil Kentaurus	Centaurus	-0.27	4.26 ly
5	Arcturus	Bootes	-0.05	36 ly
6	Vega	Lyra	+0.03	26 ly
7	Capella	Auriga	+0.08	42 ly
8	Rigel	Orion	+0.18	770 ly
9	Procyon	Canis Minor	+0.40	11.4 ly
10	Achernar	Eridanus	+0.46	143 ly

Stars and galaxies

Stars are giant balls of burning gas, mainly hydrogen, that give off their own light, which can be seen across vast distances. The 'burning' is actually nuclear fusion, whereby hydrogen is converted into helium. The hotter stars are likely to have a shorter life as they use up their fuel more quickly, but there are many factors that affect the overall life of any star. Eventually stars become unstable and either collapse or explode.

A star's absolute (intrinsic) magnitude depends on its size and temperature. The closest star to Earth (other than the Sun) is more than four light years[G] away, well outside our solar system.

Constellations[G]

Stars are grouped in the sky according to particular patterns which are named and recognised internationally. Early astronomers drew pictures from mythology around the stars as they saw them, and so created the system of constellations[G] that we have today. The far southern constellations[G] were not added until around 1751, when the Abbé de la Caille visited Cape Town and measured the positions of nearly 10,000 stars in two-and-a-half years.

Within the constellations[G], the stars were given a letter of the Greek alphabet in order of brightness. Thus the stars of the Southern Cross are Alpha, Beta, Gamma, Delta, clockwise from its long point. However, errors were made in the past, as it was not always realised that certain stars can vary in brightness over time. In Orion, for instance, you can easily see that Beta is sometimes brighter than Alpha.

Orion – the best-known constellation[w] in the sky.

17

Some constellations[G] such as the Southern Cross, Orion and the Scorpion do resemble the images they represent. But who ever heard of four stars in a square being a picture of a horse with wings (Pegasus)? Or a backward question mark being a lion? Rather than trying to see the pictures, think of the constellations[G] as geometric patterns, and you will learn to recognise them more easily. A couple of hours with a dark sky and a good star atlas will teach you to recognise at least five or six constellations[G], and probably more.

Galaxies[G]

The largest bodies we know in the universe are called galaxies[G]. These are great swirling bodies of upwards of 100,000 million suns, plus other matter in the form of gas clouds and solid debris. They take various forms: spirals, barred spirals, ellipticals and irregulars, each with its own subdivisions – but spirals are the best known. These are rather like giant catherine wheels with bright centres and spiral arms reaching out all around. Spiral galaxies can be of different sizes, but diameters in the region of 100 thousand light years[G] are common. Seen from the edge on, galaxies are quite thin and the solid debris (known as dust) can often be seen as dark lanes against them.

Our Sun is part of a galaxy[G] called the Milky Way. The Sun is about two-thirds of the way out from the centre of the Milky Way, located along one of the spiral arms. In all directions there are millions of stars, many of which form themselves into groups that we refer to as open clusters[G]. In addition there are gas clouds, which we call galactic nebulae[G]; some are hot and glowing, while others are lit up

A spiral galaxy[G], seen from an oblique angle.

A spiral galaxy^G as seen through a telescope; note the dark dust lane.

Beyond our galaxy^G

Far beyond our own galaxy^G, there are many other galaxies, but they are so distant or dispersed that we cannot detect more than three with the naked eye. These three are the two Magellanic Clouds near the south pole and the Andromeda Galaxy^G, which is the furthest object the naked eye can see, about 2.5 million light years^G away. With the use of telescopes we can see hundreds of thousands of other, fainter galaxies. The brighter ones make good targets for small amateur instruments.

by the light of stars embedded in them. However, if we look in any direction along the plane of our galaxy^G we will see a greater concentration of stars than if we look at right angles to it. When we look at the Milky Way from Earth, we are looking into our own galaxy^G.

Above and below the galactic plane is an area that contains numerous clusters of stars, gathered in a halo around the galaxy's^G centre. These clusters are of the globular type, where there are so many stars that they cannot easily be separated on photographs.

The Andromeda Galaxy^G – the furthest object that can be seen with the naked eye.

Observing the Milky Way

The Milky Way extends right around the night sky, but we can only see a portion of it at any one time. One of the best areas to observe is that part stretching from the Pointers of the Southern Cross across to Canopus. The following objects are among the most interesting in that stretch:

- Alpha Centauri is the nearest star to the Sun, and a small telescope will show it up clearly as a double star.
- Omega Centauri is the brightest globular cluster in the sky and can be found by projecting lines from the Pointers and the Southern Cross.
- Centaurus A (NGC^G 5128) is only 4° north of Omega but is difficult to find in telescopes under 150mm in diameter. It is a galaxy^G with a strong source of radio waves, and shows a very strong, dark dust lane running through it.
- The Southern Cross is quite small but with a number of bright stars. Some 40° to the north of the Cross is the distinctive Corvus, and 30° to 40° beyond that is the Virgo Cluster of galaxies and Coma Berenices.
- The Coal Sack to the southeast of the Cross is a dust cloud that hides many stars, creating the impression of a hole in the Milky Way.
- Eta Carinae is the brightest patch in the southern Milky Way and is described in more detail on page 24.
- The Diamond Cross stands out clearly and its southernmost star (Beta Carinae) can be used with Canopus (Alpha Carinae) to locate the Large Magellanic Cloud, often hard to spot from light-polluted town areas.
- The False Cross is just west of the Diamond and is similar in shape and orientation to the Southern Cross, but somewhat larger. Just beyond the foot of this cross is a magnificent open cluster^G, 0.5° in diameter (NGC^G 2516).
- Canopus is further to the west from the False Cross and is the second-brightest star in the sky. It is approximately halfway between Sirius and the South Celestial Pole – knowledge of this can help to establish direction on partly cloudy nights.

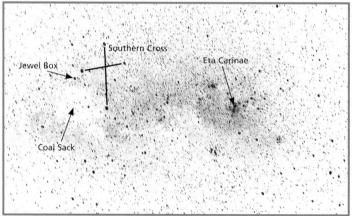

The Milky Way constitutes most of what we can see in the night skies. Almost all we can see is our own galaxy[G], made up of billions of suns, of which our own Sun is just one small member.

Seasonal skies

The dominant constellation in summer is Orion, the Hunter, which lies right across the celestial equator. In winter, the most easily recognisable is Scorpius, the scorpion, which is 15° to 40° south and can thus be almost directly overhead at the right time of night.

Summer skies

Orion is probably the best-known constellation of all, clearly visible from both hemispheres. The three bright stars of the Hunter's belt help locate many other objects in the sky (see Starhopping, page 7) and the sword scabbard running south from the centre of the belt is a fascinating region of star clusters that includes the great Orion Nebula[G].

Winter skies

Scorpius, with the bright red star Antares at its heart and with its distinctive tail, should be easy to find. At the start of the curve of the tail are three close groupings of stars in a straight line, running very nearly north-south. The most northerly one is a single star (Epsilon), the next is a double star (Mu) and the third (most southerly) is a triangle of three bright stars (Zeta) plus a fainter open cluster[G] (NGC[G] 6231). The extreme end of the tail is marked by two stars close together, and just northeast of them is the very bright open cluster[G] M7, with M6 not far away.

Sagittarius lies next to the Scorpion's tail; but far from looking like an Archer who is half horse and half man, the star pattern appears more like a teapot. Just above the teapot lid is an area that abounds in clusters and gas clouds of all colours and types. In some cases two or even three of these objects can be seen at the same time through binoculars.

Cygnus (the Swan) is also known as the Northern Cross and it stretches along the northern Milky Way in winter. It is much larger than the Southern Cross. The bright stars, Vega (west) and Altair (south), escort Cygnus across the sky, with Delphinus following close behind Altair.

Nebulae^G

Hazy patches of light in the sky are known as nebulae^G. These are massive clouds of gas, lit by hot, bright stars buried within them, and sometimes reflecting the light of nearby stars too. Emission nebulae^G release vast amounts of energy generated by member stars. Reflection nebulae^G emit no light of their own, but are illuminated only by starlight reflecting off dust. Dark nebulae^G are vast areas of gas and dust that, in the absence of stars nearby to light them, are detected only because they hide the light of more distant stars.

The Orion Nebula^G

The easiest nebula^G to spot – and which is detectable with the naked eye – is the Great Nebula^G of Orion. The second-most southerly star of the sword of Orion is actually a misty spot; with binoculars or a small telescope, it grows to a fuzzy cloud, and the larger the amplification, the more beautiful the image becomes.

The magnificent Orion Nebula^G.

Eta Carinae

Eta Carinae is a star in the constellation^G of Carina and, although it has previously been much brighter, it is presently on the borderline of naked-eye visibility. After starting to brighten in the 17th century, it continued to increase in brightness until it was equal to Sirius, the brightest star in the sky, for a short time in 1843. It then faded until 2000 when it started to brighten again.

Eta Carinae and the Keyhole Nebula^G.

NURSERIES AND GRAVEYARDS

Some nebulae^G are now known to be the birthplace of stars. The Orion Nebula^G is particularly productive, as it contains enough gas to make a cluster of thousands of stars. At its centre is a group of hot young stars, called the Trapezium, which make the surrounding gas glow so spectacularly.

Nebulae^G of another sort are formed when red giants, which are dying stars, explode and eject their outer layers of gas into space. The Crab Nebula^G resulted from a supernova, the explosive death of a massive star that was observed on Earth in 1054.

With all this renewed activity and brightening, it is possible that the star could explode as a nova and, if it does so, it could become visible in broad daylight. Some astronomers think that Eta could explode 'soon' – but by that they mean sometime in the next 3,000 or 4,000 years!

Eta is surrounded by a gas nebula^G that covers an area spanning two degrees^G, with dark dust lanes dividing it and the dark Keyhole Nebula^G in front of it all. This latter nebula^G is one of the most fascinating objects in the sky. It is comprised of opaque, non-luminous matter, and its name comes from its apparent shape. The view through a small telescope or pair of binoculars is spectacular.

The solar system

Our Sun is the centre of our solar system. Within this system are 8 planets (4 inner rocky planets, 4 outer gas giants), 3 dwarf planets, over 160 moons and more than 50,000 Small Solar System Bodies (SSSBs). The latter include the previously named asteroids[G] and countless comets in two areas known as the Kuiper Belt[G] and the Oort Cloud. All these bodies orbit the Sun, which is the only star we can see in detail because we are, relatively, so close to it.

The Sun

Our Sun is a fairly bright yellow star in which hydrogen is converted to helium by nuclear reaction. This reaction is taking place in most of the stars we can detect, although some have been discovered that are too small to support this process.

Although the Sun is immense (approximately 100 times the diameter of the Earth), it is not a solid body. Its average density is only 1.4 times that of water (as opposed to Earth's density of 5.5 times). As the Sun rotates on its axis, its equator moves faster than the poles, completing one revolution in 24.6 days compared with 34 days at the poles. This twisting effect can be detected by watching (indirectly, using safe

---

NEVER LOOK DIRECTLY AT THE SUN

Never look directly at the Sun, and particularly not through any kind of optical aid, unless specialised filters have been fitted. If you do not have a telescope, a pinhole camera can be created using a large cardboard box with a 2mm hole in one end. The image is then projected onto the opposite end of the box.

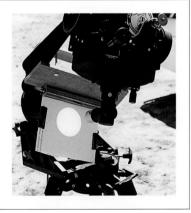

Safely projecting the sun onto a screen, using a telescope.

methods) the location of sunspots at different latitudes as they make their way across the Sun.

Sunspots are dark areas on the photosphere, which is what we call the bright surface of the Sun. They are caused by a magnetic effect below the surface and can be of varying sizes. The central, darkest area (umbra) is surrounded by a lighter area (penumbra), and sometimes several umbrae will share one large penumbra.

Solar observers count individual spots as well as the number of groups. With highly specialised filters it is possible to see flares and other activity.

Solar eclipse

Sometimes the Moon comes between the Sun and the Earth causing a solar eclipse, which can be seen over a large area, although the Sun will only be totally obscured from a narrow band across the Earth's surface, and then for only a few minutes. Total eclipses are a magical experience and thousands of people travel vast distances to see them.

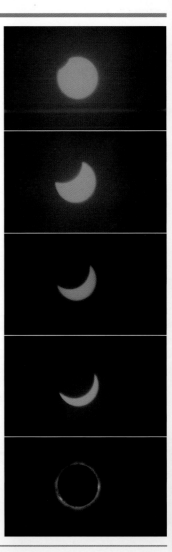

The various stages of a solar eclipse, from First Contact (top) to complete coverage, or Totality.

26

The Moon

Our nearest natural neighbour in space is the Moon, which is easily observed with the naked eye or binoculars. The Moon is so fascinating that it can become the subject of a life's work.

With the naked eye, maria (seas) can easily be seen on the Moon. These were formed by volcanic activity, where lava spread out over the surface, sometimes engulfing earlier craters whose shapes can still be seen faintly. Using binoculars, the first thing to strike the viewer is the number of craters of various sizes on the Moon's surface. In some cases, new craters have formed in the maria or on top of earlier craters, creating intricate patterns. The craters were formed about 4,000 million years ago by impacts during a bombardment by meteors[G]. Change on the surface continues, in the form of landslides in the crater walls and among the mountains.

The best time to observe the Moon is around first quarter, when sunlight illuminates it at 90 degrees[G] to the observer's line of sight. (The same situation

Full Moon – as seen through binoculars.

occurs at last quarter, but observing it then means being up at 3 a.m!). In this position, the mountains and crater walls cast dark shadows, so that the features stand out in sharp relief and can be seen more easily.

Although the same side of the Moon always faces Earth, small east-west and north-south variations do take place, allowing an occasional glimpse of the fringes of the mysterious far side.

Lunar eclipse

Lunar eclipses (when the Earth passes between the Sun and the Moon) can be seen every few years from almost any location and offer a change from normal lunar observations. As the Moon enters the shadow of the Earth, it does not lose all illumination because sunlight is scattered by the Earth's atmosphere, producing a coppery colour on the Moon. The intensity of this colour is different for each eclipse.

> The Sun is 400 times the diameter of the Moon but it is 400 times as far away so they appear the same size in the sky. The Sun is also 400,000 times brighter.

Total eclipse of the Moon – light filtered by the Earth's atmosphere casts a warm, rosy glow on the Moon's surface.

The planets

Nearest to the Sun are the rocky planets, Mercury, Venus, Earth and Mars; followed by the gas giants Jupiter, Saturn, Uranus and Neptune. Details of when it is convenient or ideal to observe any of the planets can be found in astronomical handbooks (see 'Further reading' on page 55). This is especially important for Mercury and Venus, which can be seen in either the evening or the morning sky, but which are not visible throughout the night. (Do not rely on northern hemisphere magazines for this purpose, as the northern and southern aspects do not coincide, especially near midsummer or midwinter.)

The planets further out than Earth work their way across the sky from west to east against the starry background as the days progress, but because of an optical illusion, they seem to reverse direction shortly before they reach opposition (the point at which the planet,

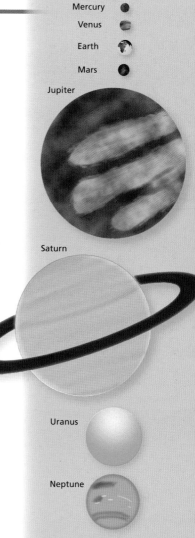

Sun

Mercury

Venus

Earth

Mars

Jupiter

Saturn

Uranus

Neptune

Relative sizes of the Sun and planets.

the Earth and the Sun are all aligned) and go backwards for a time until they again start moving eastwards. The turning points and distances covered in retrograde motion vary with the planet and the inclination of its orbit, but dates of stationary points are to be found in annual astronomical handbooks.

With the exception of Mercury and Venus, all the planets have at least one moon, and most have many more.

Almost all the planets can be seen with binoculars, but you will need to consult a guide chart before you will be able to identify Uranus and Neptune in the sky.

The planets – table of facts

	Distance from Sun: 10^6 km	Period of revolution: years	Mass: (Earth = 1)	Equatorial diameter: 10^3 km	Rotation period	Inclination of equator to orbit	No. of known satellites
Mercury	58	0,24	0,055	4,88	58,65d	0°	0
Venus	108	0,62	0,815	12,10	243d	178°	0
Earth	150	1,00	1,000	12,76	23h56m	23°27'	1
Mars	228	1,88	0,107	6,79	24h37m	23°59'	2
Jupiter	778	11,9	318,867	142,98	09h51m	03°04'	64
Saturn	1,429	29,5	95,142	120,54	10h14m	26°44'	62
Uranus	2,871	84,0	14,559	51,12	17,2h	97°52'	27
Neptune	4,504	164,8	17,207	49,53	17,8h	29°34'	14

The inner planets

The four innermost planets, Mercury, Venus, Earth and Mars, are all relatively small and have rocky surfaces.

Mercury and Venus: The two planets closer to the Sun than the Earth can only be seen in the evening or morning sky and although they appear to travel away from the Sun, they soon move back towards it again. Orbiting as they do between Earth and the Sun, the maximum separation between the Sun and these planets as seen from Earth is 47° for Venus but only 28° for Mercury. Their maximum magnitudes are -4.4 (Venus) and -1.9 (Mercury), at which times they are brighter than any star.

Venus and Mercury both show phases (like our Moon), which can be viewed with a small telescope. It is also possible to see Venus with the naked eye in broad daylight when it is at its brightest, but you may need to locate it with binoculars first. If you do this, it is wise to stand just in the shade of a building so that there is no danger of accidentally pointing the binoculars at the Sun while searching the sky.

Earth: It is the densest body in our solar system and the only one with an atmosphere that can support life as we know it.

Mars: There is currently much interest in Mars, as it is the next target for major space

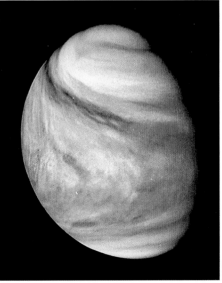

Venus, the evening star.

NASA

exploration. This is hoped to culminate in a manned probe to the planet, which will no doubt be well covered by the media.

Mars may be unspectacular when seen through small telescopes, but is nevertheless very bright – as bright as -2.8 at its best. It is a rust-orange colour and often displays polar icecaps, which grow and shrink with the seasons. For surface details, a fairly large instrument is usually needed, although occasional planet-wide dust storms can be detected with smaller telescopes.

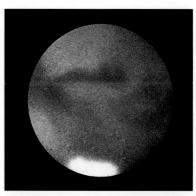

Mars, the red planet.

Mars is home to the largest volcano in the solar system (Olympus Mons, 24,000m high) and its surface shows signs of water having been present in the past. Moving water-soaked salts have recently been detected during warmer months, when temperatures reach about -23°C (salt lowers the freezing point of water).

Its two moons, Phobos and Deimos, are both too small to be easily seen in amateur telescopes. Phobos orbits Mars much faster than Mars turns on its axis, while

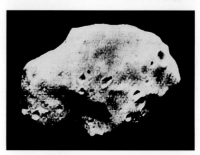

Phobos, one of Mars' moons, as photographed from a spacecraft and showing detail that would never be visible from the Earth. Most amateur telescopes cannot detect Mars' moons at all.

Deimos is slower, so that from the Mars surface, the two moons would appear to orbit in different directions – Phobos eastwards and Deimos to the west.

THE ASTEROIDS[G] (NOW CLASSIFIED AS SSSBs)

An asteroid[G] is like a really small planet: a solid body that is in orbit around the Sun. The thousands of asteroids could be the dismembered parts of a planet that never formed properly, but this is by no means certain and is only one theory that has been put forward over the years. Most of the asteroids[G] are between the orbits of Mars and Jupiter, although there are a number well outside these limits. There are about 50 that are magnitude 11 or brighter, and should therefore be visible in 50mm binoculars, but one needs specially prepared finding charts to be able to locate them.

Because they are so small, it is difficult even to define their shape and size in relation to the amount of light they reflect. However, occasionally one passes in front of a distant star and blots out its light for a short time.

The timing of these occultations[G] by amateurs is currently the best way to measure the actual dimensions of these asteroids[G]. If more than one observer records disappearance and reappearance times for the event, it is possible to construct a drawing of the probable shape of the asteroid[G] even though it is too small to be clearly seen through a telescope. The drawing then reflects the shape of the asteroid[G] recorded this way by the different observers.

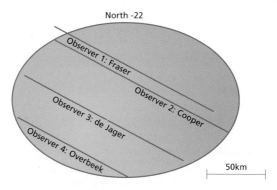

Actual results of an observation of 48 Doris made by South African amateurs, led by Danie Overbeek, on 14 October 1999. This particular asteroid was found to be 107km by 267km.

Drawing courtesy of the late Danie Overbeek and MNASSA

The outer planets

The second group of four planets, Jupiter, Saturn, Uranus and Neptune, do not have hard surfaces like the smaller inner ones. These are great, spinning balls of gas, showing varying levels of surface detail in small telescopes. In common with the Sun, their equators revolve faster than their poles, and in some cases this produces violently turbulent effects on their surfaces.

Jupiter: This planet is the amateur's favourite. Jupiter shows changes in the appearance of its cloud patterns, and records of such changes are kept by various astronomical societies around the world. Jupiter's brightness is surpassed only by that of the Sun, the Moon and Venus, its maximum magnitude being about -2.6.

Four of Jupiter's moons (discovered by Galileo) are easily seen, and as we view the system from its edge, the moons pass in front of or behind the planet between their trips out to either side. It was largely Galileo's views of Jupiter through his small telescope that convinced him that the Sun, not the Earth, was the centre of our solar system. He realised that the moons were in fact travelling in near circular orbits and he timed their periods. These four bright moons, Io, Europa, Ganymede and Callisto, are now jointly referred to as the Galilean moons. Most astronomical annual handbooks give predictions of events pertaining to these moons.

The equatorial bands and the four Galilean moons are always there to be seen, but some of the fainter moons and less prominent bands are only apparent under good sky conditions.

Jupiter – Pioneer 10 image.

NASA

Saturn: This is probably the most easily recognisable planet because of its very obvious ring system – the planet that brings the greatest squeals of delight from observatory visitors. The three rings seen from Earth are revealed to be about a hundred rings when photographed from a spacecraft with the sunlight behind them.

Saturn's rings – Pioneer 10 image.

As Saturn and Earth move around their orbits, they change their relative positions, so that we sometimes see the north surface of the rings and sometimes the south. Between the two extremes, the rings, which are very thin, have varying angles to our line of sight, and when they are edge-on to us (or edge-on to the Sun so that no light falls on them), they become invisible in small telescopes. It is quite a shock to see Saturn without its rings. The rings will next line up with the Sun, which will render them invisible, on 5 May 2025.

Saturn has a maximum magnitude of -0.3. The second largest of all the planets, Saturn has less than one-third the mass of Jupiter, but still more than five times the mass of Neptune and six times that of Uranus. Saturn has many moons but only a few can be easily detected. Titan is the brightest at magnitude 8.3, with Rhea much fainter at 9.7.

Uranus and Neptune: It is impossible for the average amateur astronomer to observe the two most distant planets in detail. There is satisfaction in simply being able to locate them with the help of sky charts.

Uranus can be seen with the naked eye, but is easier to find with binoculars. It has a greenish colour and appears quite different from the stars, it is not difficult to identify once you have a finder chart. Its moons are beyond the capabilities of telescopes of less than 20cm diameter.

Uranus reaches opposition (when it is in line with and nearest to Earth) about four or five days later each year. It can reach a magnitude of 6 (the limit of naked-eye visibility).

Neptune is fainter than Uranus, never exceeding magnitude 7.7. Its disc, as seen from Earth, is only two seconds^G of arc in diameter. Neptune's discovery on 23 September 1846 was the direct result of calculations based on its gravitational effect on the orbit of Uranus. Its atmosphere contains a relatively high percentage (2%) of methane gas, which absorbs red light, so that the planet appears slightly blue when viewed through a telescope. Neptune's system of rings was first discovered by observations from the Voyager 2 spacecraft in 1989.

An artist's impression of Uranus and Miranda, one of its moons.

NASA

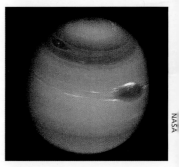

Neptune, the blue planet.

NASA

Small Solar System Bodies (SSSBs)

With the discovery of more bodies far out in the solar system, the International Astronomical Union had to redefine the various types of object in orbit around our Sun. It did this in August 2006 by (1) reducing the number of planets from nine to eight, (2) introducing 'dwarf planets' (Pluto, Ceres and Eris) and (3) deciding that all other bodies, except satellites, orbiting the Sun should be called SSSBs. There will probably be further amendments to the definitions in future, but the basic pattern now seems established.

Comets

Comets are like 'dirty snowballs' – lumps of ice embedded with dirt and gas. Most are unspectacular and appear as small blots of light. At times they can be impressive and appear in the sky with a long bright tail. Most of these wanderers of the solar system travel in elliptical orbits, which take them far from the Sun and out of our sight.

The Sun is one of the foci of the elliptical orbits and these comets perpetually return to the vicinity of the Sun. However, they have very little mass compared with other solar system objects and they are notoriously unpredictable as regards their brightness.

During their visits to the Sun, comets melt and so lose some of their mass in a cloud of dust and gas known as a coma. This coma may be pushed out by the Sun's radiation to form one, two or (in rare cases) even more tails.

Although these bodies have little or no effect on Earth, there is still the possibility that one could strike us and cause catastrophic damage. In July 1994, Comet Shoemaker-Levy 9 crashed into Jupiter and the impacts left large impressions on Jupiter's surface. If a comet of comparable size were to hit the Earth (some ten times smaller than Jupiter), the results can only be imagined.

Bright naked-eye comets are named for their discoverers or those who calculated their orbits. Among recent bright comets are Comet Bennett, discovered by the late Jack Bennett of Pretoria in 1970, Comet Hale-Bopp, jointly discovered in 1995 and Comet McNaught, which was magnificent early in 2007.

Comet Hale-Bopp of 1997, seen from Selsey on the south coast of England.

Meteors^G

Commonly known as shooting stars, meteors^G are not really stars at all, but small pieces of debris left behind by comets and spread out along their orbits. This debris is attracted by Earth's gravity and so enters the Earth's atmosphere, where it burns up.

Because a meteor^G shower comes from a single direction, it appears that the trails all radiate from one spot in the sky (called the radiant) and we give the shower the name of the constellation^G where that spot is located. Meteor^G showers can be fast or slow, and some leave sparks or smoke trails. Some are very bright ('fireballs'), others quite faint and you need a dark sky to see them well. Some are so big that they do not fully burn up in the Earth's atmosphere and they fall to Earth as meteorites^G.

Because meteors^G move so fast and are visible for only a second or two, most meteor^G observing is done with the naked eye. Once the radiant is located, it is best to watch the sky about 30° to 40° to left or right of it, about 50° above the horizon. Meteors^G close to the radiant will be travelling almost directly towards us and will only show short trails or sometimes just single spots of light.

As the Earth spins on its axis, it is also moving along its orbit around the Sun. In the early hours of the morning, as the observer's line of longitude starts to rotate towards the Sun, he is facing in the direction of the Earth's orbit. This is where meteors^G are colliding with our atmosphere, so we are more likely to see meteors^G at this time.

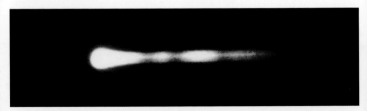

A Leonid meteor^G, here seen breaking up as it enters the Earth's atmosphere.

Advanced stargazing

Once novice astronomers have a reasonable knowledge of the sky, know their way around and can find examples of the various types of objects, the subject is wide open to progress in a whole variety of directions. **Comet observing** is usually combined with some other interest, to keep one busy when the comets are faint. Some observers with plenty of patience carry out regular searches to try to find new comets, sometimes for years without success, but the thrill of being the first to discover a new one makes it worthwhile. Observations of known comets are made to record the size and appearance of the head (coma), the length and direction of any tail and any change in appearance.

Deep-sky observers will try to locate all the objects in the Messier catalogue, compiled by Charles Messier and identifying over 100 objects that could be mistaken for comets. These objects are numbered M1, M2, M3, etc., and include distant galaxies, gaseous nebulae[G] and clusters of stars. Although compiled

The Horsehead Nebula[G] can be quite hard to see, and requires a dark sky and at least a 200mm telescope.

in the northern hemisphere, many of its entries are visible from the south. There are two further, similar catalogues: the Bennett list was compiled by Pretoria comet-seeker Jack Bennett, and identifies southern objects that might resemble comets in areas not covered by Messier; and well-known author and broadcaster, Sir Patrick Moore, compiled a more comprehensive list covering both hemispheres, known as the Caldwell catalogue.

Double-star observing is another rewarding activity. There are more double stars than single ones, but many are too close together to be clearly distinguished through telescopes. However, many of the nearer and brighter ones have never been observed sufficiently to determine whether they are truly together in space or whether they are just in the same line of sight. If they are orbiting each other, the period of the orbits needs to be measured. There is much work to be done.

Meteor^G observing requires no equipment other than a pen and paper to record the time, brightness, colour and speed of those seen. Sightings are reported to the meteor^G sections of various societies and together provide valuable information; this is probably the easiest way to enter the field of serious observing. Displays seen can be beautiful, and sometimes spectacular – with meteors brighter than magnitude -3 (about the same as Venus near its brightest) being classified as fireballs.

STAR PARTIES

Star parties consist of a group of astronomers getting together and setting up their telescopes for anyone to look through. The astronomers themselves try out each other's equipment and the general public is welcome to come and have a look and ask questions. These are probably the best way to encourage interest in the subject and have been the starting point for many of today's leading amateurs and professionals. The size of these events varies. Sometimes there are only three or four telescopes in use, but at least one party in the USA attracts over 1 000 people every year.

South Africa's Sutherland Observatory, where conditions for observing are among the best in the world.

Star charts

The star charts that follow represent the entire night sky at 21:00 local time on the 15th day of each month. Earlier in the evening or earlier in the month, the stars will be further east, and later than these times, they will be further west. The names of bright stars are shown in italics, and constellations are identified by their official three-letter abbreviations to which a key can be found on the inside front cover.

How to use the charts: Turn the chart so that the compass direction in which you are facing is at the bottom. If you then lift the chart in front of your face and further upwards until it is above your head, it will show the entire sky with the overhead point in its centre. This position is uncomfortable, so it is easier to hold the chart in front of you and use only the lower half in which the edge of the chart represents the horizon and the centre is overhead. As you turn to your right, so the chart should be rotated clockwise (or vice versa) to keep the correct compass direction at the bottom.

January

The ecliptic shows the approximate yearly path of the Sun, Moon and planets.

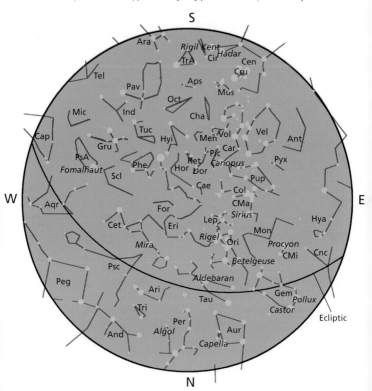

Pleiades: Large open cluster[G] in Taurus, visible with naked eye or binoculars.

Hyades: The face of Taurus the Bull with bright red Aldebaran as the eye.

Orion Constellation: Straddles the equator; western star of the belt is right above the equator. Orion Nebula: In the sword scabbard above the belt; looks impressive through a small telescope.

February

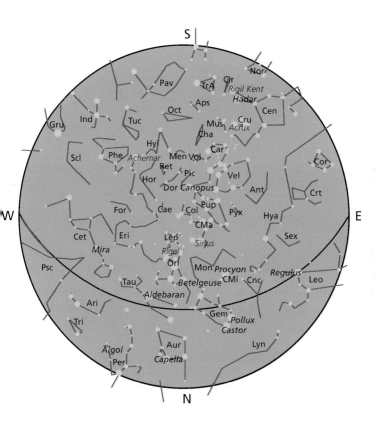

Rigel and **Betelgeuse:** Brightest stars in Orion. Betelgeuse is variable[G] so it can be brighter or fainter than Rigel. Compare them regularly.
Acrux and **Achernar:** Equidistant on opposite sides of the South Celestial Pole.

March

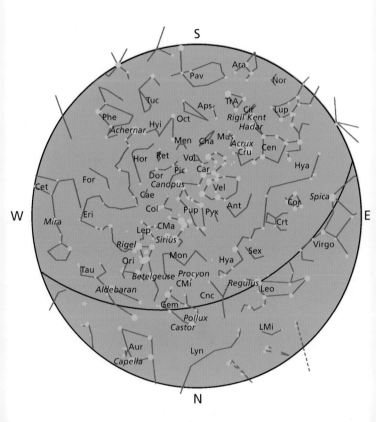

False Cross: Open cluster^G at the bottom of this cross; best viewed through a telescope.

Sirius: Brightest star in the sky – Orion's belt points to it.

Gemini Constellation: NE of Orion with bright stars Castor and Pollux.

April

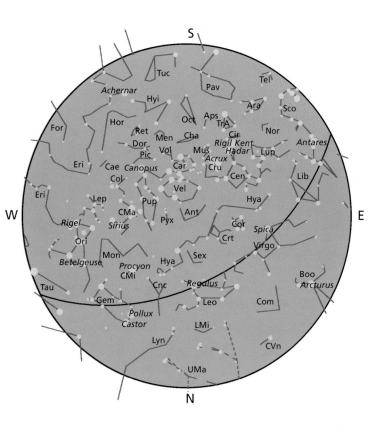

Leo: Appears like an upside-down question mark in the north.
Alpha Centauri: Nearest star to the Sun. Shows double in small telescopes. Also known as Rigil Kentaurus.

May

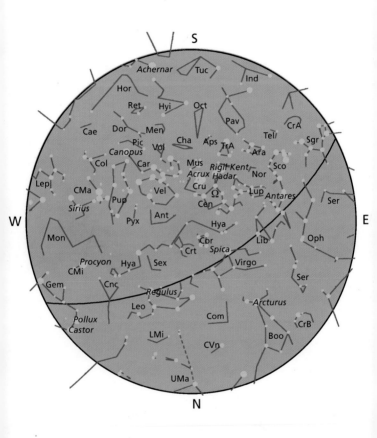

Milky Way: High in the south. Looking through binoculars is very rewarding.
Omega Centauri (Ω): Largest and brightest globular cluster in the sky.
Arcturus: Bright star rising in NE.

June

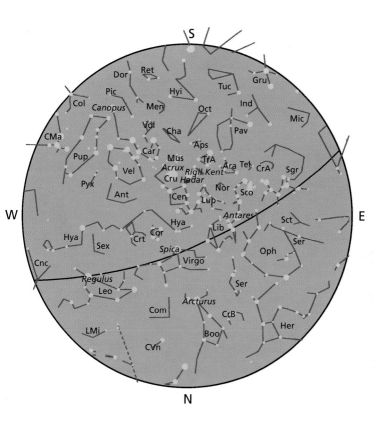

Corona Borealis: Northern Crown rising soon after Arcturus.
Scorpius: The curved tail is full of interest and ends near the centre of the galaxy[G]. Many clusters can be seen through binoculars or a telescope.
Antares: Bright red star at the heart of Scorpius.

July

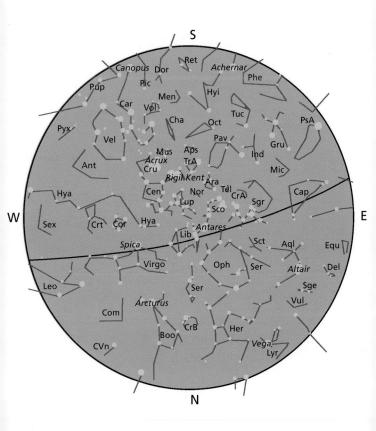

Sagittarius: East of Scorpius, identify the 'teapot' – see page 22.
Vega: Bright northern hemisphere star, low in the northeast.

August

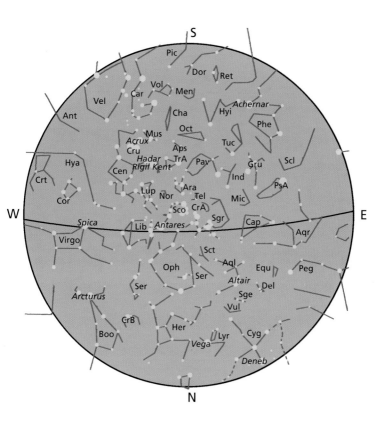

Altair: Find this northern bright star in Aquila, the Eagle.
Southern Cross (Crux): Now well towards the SW.
Achernar: Rising in SE.
Scorpius: Still overhead, the Milky Way now almost running south to north.

September

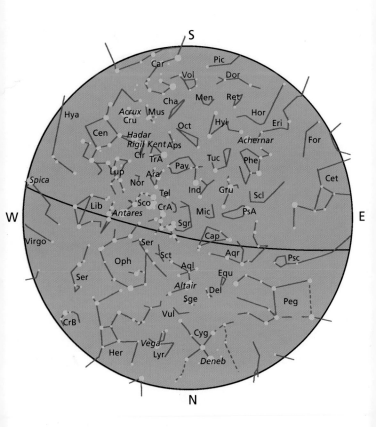

Cygnus the Swan, or **Northern Cross:** Low in the northern Milky Way. Note the **South Pole** is almost exactly halfway between Achernar and Acrux in the Southern Cross (see page 15).

October

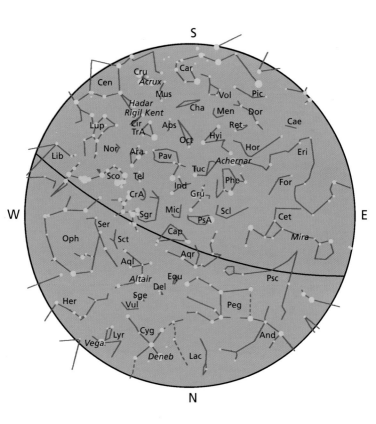

Pegasus: Four stars appear in a large square in the NE.
Southern Cross (Crux): Almost on the horizon, just west of south.
Canopus: Rising in SE, showing summer is on the way.

November

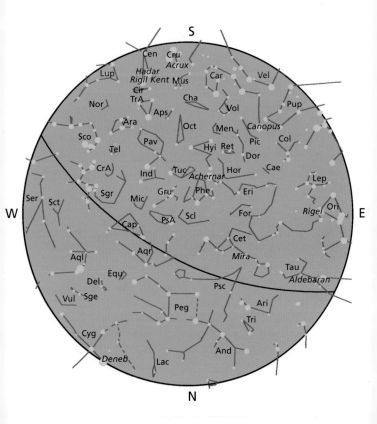

Scorpius: Now almost set, and Orion starting to rise.
Andromeda: Low in the north to the west of Pegasus, with the galaxy[G] visible through binoculars in a dark sky.

December

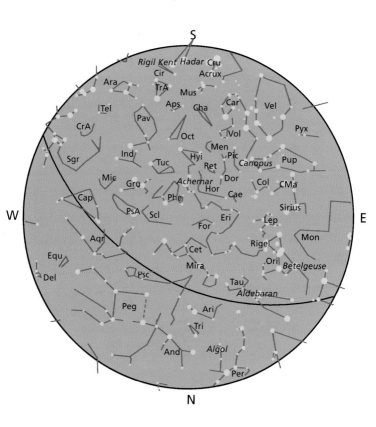

Pleiades: Large open cluster^G in Taurus; can be seen with the naked eye or through binoculars.
Hyades: The face of Taurus the Bull, with bright red Aldebaran as the eye.

Clubs and observatories

Clubs and societies

- Astronomical Society of SA
  PO Box 9, Observatory, 7935
  assa.saao.ac.za
  Local centres exist in seven towns
  and cities around southern
  Africa, and hold meetings
  monthly or more frequently.
- Friends of Boyden Observatory
  PO Box 13004, Brandhof, 9324
- Port Elizabeth People's
  Observatory Society
  PO Box 7988, PE, 6055

Observatories open to the public

- SA Astronomical Observatory
  Observatory Road,
  Observatory 7935, Cape Town
  Tel: (021) 447 0025
  www.saao.ac.za
  Open: 20:00 on 2nd Saturday
  each month. Parties of more
  than 12 must phone to book.
- SAAO Sutherland Visitors
  Centre now open; day or night
  visits can be arranged. Phone
  (023) 571 2436 for details and
  bookings. Sutherland Tourism
  Office: (023) 571 1265.

- Boyden Observatory
  Bloemfontein
  Contact Dr MJH Hoffman
  Tel: (051) 401 2924
  hoffmamj.sci@ufs.ac.za
- Cederberg Observatory
  Dwarsrivier, PO Cederberg
  Open Saturday evening on
  most weekends.
  Operated by seven
  amateur astronomers.
  Tel: (021) 913 4200
  **www.cederbergobservatory.
  org.za**
- Hartebeesthoek Radio
  Astronomy Observatory
  Visiting days once a month
  on Sundays at 15:00.
  Essential to book:
  Tel: (012) 326 0742
  weekdays between
  09:00 and 12:00.
- Port Elizabeth People's
  Observatory
  cnr Westview Drive &
  MacFarlane Rd, Port Elizabeth
  Open 1st and 3rd Wednesday
  every month and every
  Wednesday during December
  and January.

Further reading

Arnold, HJP, Doherty, P, Moore, P. *Photographic Atlas of the Stars*. Institute of Physics Publishing Inc., Bristol & Philadelphia.

Fairall, A. *Starwatching*. Struik Nature (Penguin Random House), Cape Town.

Fairall, A. *Starwise*. Struik Nature (Penguin Random House), Cape Town.

Jansen, A. *Star Maps for Southern Africa*. Struik Nature (Penguin Random House), Cape Town.

Levy, DH. *Skywatching*. Harper Collins Publishers, London.

Moore, P. *Exploring the Night Sky with Binoculars*. Cambridge University Press, Cambridge.

Redpath, I. *Norton's Star Atlas*. Longman Scientific & Technical.

Slotegraaf, A. (ed.). *2016 Sky Guide Africa South. Astronomical Handbook for Southern Africa*. Astronomical Society of Southern Africa (ASSA) / Struik Nature (Penguin Random House), Cape Town.

Tirion, W. *Cambridge Star Atlas*. Cambridge University Press, Cambridge.

Useful websites

These constantly change, but an up-to-date list appears in the ASSA handbook, *Sky Guide Africa South*, every year.

Glossary

Asteroids: Minor planets, most of which orbit the Sun between the paths of Mars and Jupiter.

Conjunction: the position of a planet when it is in line with the Sun as seen from Earth.

Constellations: Groups of stars and other objects forming patterns that have been internationally recognised.

Degree: One 360th part of a circle.

Galaxy: Very large system of stars held together by gravity and containing many millions of stars and other matter.

Globular clusters: Concentrated groups of many stars found above and below the plane of a galaxy.

Kuiper belt: A belt of asteroids beyond Neptune's orbit that is probably a source of short-period comets.

Glossary (cont.)

Light year: The distance travelled by light in one earth year at 299,792.5km per second (often approximated to 300,000km per second). See also Parsec.

Magnification: The amount by which an optical instrument enlarges an object. In a telescope, degree of magnification is given by dividing the focal length (the distance from a lens or curved mirror at which parallel rays of light are brought to a point) of the main lens or mirror by the focal length of the eyepiece.

Meteor: Tiny fragment of matter burning up in the Earth's atmosphere, usually at an altitude of about 100km.

Meteorite: Unusually large meteor that does not fully burn up in the atmosphere and survives to strike the Earth.

Minute: One 60th part of a degree (arc) or of an hour (time).

Nebula: A cloud of dust and gas in space. This name was once also applied to distant galaxies, e.g. Andromeda 'Nebula'.

NGC: New General Catalogue.

Occultation: The obscuring of a star or planet by an intervening body, usually the Moon.

Oort cloud: A supposed shell of comets around the solar system 1,000 to 2,000 times as far out as Neptune.

Open cluster: A cluster of stars in the galactic plane of our galaxy.

Opposition: the position of an outer planet when it is opposite the Sun as seen from the Earth and is approximately at its nearest to the Earth.

Parsec: Unit of distance equal to 3.26 light years.

Second: One 60th part of a minute (of arc or of time).

Variable stars: Stars with varying brightness, either regular or irregular.